Focus on Famous Women

Billie Jean King
Queen of the Courts

CAROL BAUER CHURCH

Greenhaven Press, Inc.

1611 POLK ST. N.E. MINNEAPOLIS, MINNESOTA 55413

53557

PHOTOGRAPHIC CREDITS

Betty Moffitt: 7, 9, 10, 36.
Wide World Photos: 5, 15, 18, 19, 22, 27, 30, 33, 34, 37, 39, 41, 43, 47, 53, bottom of 54, 55, 57, 59, 60, 62.
UPI: cover, 2, 24, 31, 40, 44, 45, 50, 51, top of 54, 64, 65, 66-67.

© 1976 by Greenhaven Press, Inc.
ISBN 0-912616-41-5

81-14069

Table of Contents

Billie Jean King

Queen of the Courts

Introduction

Billie Jean's first tournament! She was very excited. For the occasion her mother made a neat pair of white shorts which Billie Jean wore with a white T-shirt.

After the tournament, a photographer got the players together for a picture.

"Sorry, Honey," he said to Billie Jean. "You're not dressed properly, so you can't be in the picture."

"What?" Billie Jean asked.

"You're wearing shorts, and rules say girls must wear tennis dresses."

Billie Jean did not even own a tennis dress. Tears welled up in her eyes as she stepped away from the group. She fought hard to keep from crying as she watched the others pose together for the picture.

Eleven year old Billie Jean decided then and there that someday she would change the rules of tennis. She did not like the taste of discrimination she had just received.

Chapter 1

Beginnings

Bill and Betty Moffitt's only daughter was born on November 22, 1943. She was named Billie Jean for her father, a Navy man serving in World War II.

Even as a young child in sunny Long Beach, California, Billie Jean took things more seriously than most children her age. From her earliest years she had a curious longing to travel and find out about people in other countries. A feeling deep inside told her that she was going to do something very special with her life.

"Tom boy" is the name given to girls who happen to like sports better than little girl things. Billie Jean was a tom boy. She liked playing softball, basketball, and football, and she played very well. On a boy's football team, she helped win a game with a long field goal. Not bad for a girl. Not bad for a boy either. In basketball she was taken off the team because she often made so many points in a game that her teammates became jealous. At age ten, as the youngest player, she helped her team win the Long Beach softball championship. As her football career was advancing especially well, her mother decided to call it to a quick halt. She did not like raising a lady halfback.

Billie Jean Moffitt, age five, holding brother Randy

"Choose a more feminine sport," her mother suggested, "one in which you can still be a lady."

But what? Her dad loved sports and had taught her most of what she already knew. He suggested that she try swimming, golf, or tennis.

Billie Jean did not want to spend the rest of her life in a swimming pool. Golf? What a drag. It was much too slow for her. Tennis? Maybe.

"What's it like, Dad?" she asked.

"Well, you hit a ball and run a lot," he answered.

Billie Jean decided to give it a try.

A racquet cost eight dollars. Because the Moffitts never had money to spare, Billie Jean went around the neighborhood doing odd jobs, earning fifty cents here, a quarter there, until she had enough to buy the racquet. Then she was on her way.

The first time she tried, she could not even hit the ball, and she was frustrated. She needed lessons in tennis.

6

Billie Jean serious about her tennis at age eleven

Talking tennis with friend Darlene Hard

At the public parks in Long Beach, Mr. Clyde Walker (then over sixty years old) was giving tennis lessons. He had taught at private clubs, but he changed to public parks. Kids in the parks seemed to come because they really wanted to, not because their parents were forcing them. The day Billie Jean had her first lesson, she was five feet four inches tall, 125 pounds, and only ten years old. Mr. Walker taught her how to hit the ball, and immediately Billie Jean knew she would love tennis.

"How was it?" her mother asked as Billie Jean rushed breathlessly into the kitchen after the first day.

"Great. Absolutely great! Mother, I'm going to become the best tennis player in the whole world."

"That's fine," her mother replied. "I know you will be good at it."

8

The Moffitt home held a closely-knit family. Billie Jean's only brother, Randy, was born in 1948. Neatness, discipline, patriotism, and right and wrong were clearly spelled out. Bill and Betty instilled in their children a desire to win.

Bill would say, "Any day of any week there is always somebody better around."

Each day their mother drove the children to the parks where Billie Jean played tennis, and Randy played baseball. Randy later became a pitcher for the San Francisco Giants.

Working on her forehand

In her first tournament at age eleven, Billie Jean had a taste of what she was to be up against in the future. She wore a lovely, neat looking pair of white shorts made by her mother. Because of a rule that girls were to wear tennis dresses, she was not allowed to be in a photograph of the players taken at the end of the tournament. Billie Jean did not even own a tennis dress!

This left a deep impression on the eleven year old, and she decided then and there that someday she would make some changes in tennis.

Tennis

Tennis had been played for hundreds of years before Billie Jean discovered it. In the courts of Persia and in the castles of the Middle Ages, it was first played with a hand glove, then with a paddle, and later with a racquet. From the very earliest times, tennis had been associated with the upper classes. Rules and etiquette surrounding the game were very strict and prissy: only white could be worn; no one could shout at matches; only polite quiet applause was allowed. Too bad that such a marvelous sport as tennis was surrounded with such stuffiness.

Practice was important, so Billie Jean used every spare minute to improve her game. Mr. Walker taught her that the purpose of tennis was to keep hitting the ball over the net while outlasting your opponent. He taught that a good stroke depends on how much of your body's power you can put into it. The harder you hit, the less time your opponent has to react. As in all sports, knowing your opponent's weaknesses and strengths is also important. Billie Jean was to be often reminded of this. Mind and thoughts also influence one's game. If a person is confused, frightened, or in conflict, she may not be able to play a good game.

Her mother was not happy to see Billie Jean devoting so much time to tennis that she was skipping her piano practice. Soon Billie Jean began winning tournaments in Long Beach, earning the first of her many trophies.

From the very beginning, she loved to win. But Billie Jean knew that she could also learn from her losses. After studying and thinking about her mistakes, she worked to correct them one by one. She knew that constant and steady improvement were necessary if she was to reach her goal of being the number one tennis player in the whole world.

3

The Holy Ground of Wimbledon

Her teen years were spent practicing, winning, and losing tennis matches. At age sixteen she began taking lessons from Alice Marble, a tennis champion who, among other honors, had shared the mixed doubles crown of Wimbledon in 1939 with a Mr. Bobby Riggs. (We will hear more of him later.) With her drive and practice, Billie Jean improved so much that she was accepted as an entry in the tournament at Wimbledon, England, considered to be **the** event of tennis.

The year was 1961, and Billie Jean was a senior in high school. If she went to Wimbledon, she would miss her graduation exercises. But she had no trouble deciding what to do. She chose Wimbledon!

Little Miss Moffitt soon found herself on what was considered almost holy ground at Wimbledon. Wimbledon was the place where the first tennis tournament was held in 1877. Each year players from forty countries went there to compete for honors. Wimbledon was surrounded with prestige, color, and history. All serious tennis players dreamed of winning Wimbledon titles and having their names inscribed on a shield along with those of other winners.

Playing at Wimbledon for the first time in 1961

Five championships are determined at Wimbledon: **mixed doubles** where a man and woman play another man and woman; **men's doubles** where two men play two other men; **women's doubles** where two women play two other women; **men's singles** where one man plays another man; and **women's singles** where one woman plays another woman.

As in all important tournaments, the best players are matched or "seeded" with the less skilled players in the first round. It is always a great accomplishment to reach the quarter finals, the semifinals, and the finals. The winners of the finals are considered tops in the world.

That first year at Wimbledon was quite an experience for Billie Jean Moffitt. She and Karen Hantze were the youngest players ever to win the women's doubles crown. But in the singles playoff, she didn't fare so well. As a matter of fact, she was defeated in the very first round.

14

4

A Surprising Upset

Billie Jean went home making plans to improve her game. At Wimbledon she had seen great tennis players in action, and her desire to be **number one** became even stronger. She won a few small United States tournaments that year of 1961, but none very spectacular.

Billie Jean returned in 1962 for the yearly Wimbledon tournaments. She found herself playing against the number one or top ''seed,'' Margaret Smith of Australia. Margaret, 5 feet 10 inches tall, had not lost a game in ten months, and had won important titles in Australia, France, and Italy. Everyone expected her to win at Wimbledon and later in the United States Open at Forest Hills, New York.

''No one can beat Margaret Smith,'' everyone was saying.

16

She was about to have a grand slam year, winning all
the important tournaments in the world — so people
thought.

But Billie Jean came on the scene, chunky, five feet six
inches tall, 135 pounds, wearing blue rhinestone-trimmed
glasses because she was almost blind without them, and
ranked only third among the United States women.

In a match meant to be a snap for the champion,
Margaret started out strong, winning the first set of
games. Billie Jean was worried. But with several
well-placed shots, Billie Jean won the second set. The
18,000 spectators were amazed. The gal from Australia
built up a lead 4-1, and things looked good for her. With
the determination and skill which were later to be her
trademarks, Billie Jean held Margaret's score to 5 while
bringing her own up to 6. Then she clinched the final set
with a shot that left Margaret amazed and out of touch.

Playing champion Margaret Smith at Wimbledon, 1962

18

With Margaret Smith after spectacular upset, 1962

Victory for Billie Jean! And what a victory! Never had the top woman been defeated by an unknown player in the first round of games. The event was termed the most spectacular upset in the history of Wimbledon.

Billie Jean who had been shouting to herself throughout the match, saying, "Stay in there, Billie!" and "Pour it on!" threw her racquet into the air and danced toward the net.

"This is the biggest thrill of my life, but I have never been so nervous," she exclaimed.

After losing in one of the later rounds, she said, "I've got a long way to go if I'm going to be really good."

She went home to California to practice.

Back at Wimbledon in 1963, Jilly Bean, as she was called on her Los Angeles State College tennis team, was still overweight, (she loved ice cream), colorful, loud, tense, and scared. She had gained a reputation for her endless shouting, laughing, clowning, running, and winning. That year she made it to the finals, defeating women seeded second, third, and seventh. Her opponent in the final match was again Margaret Smith, still known as the world's best woman tennis player. Margaret was about to make up for the loss to Billie Jean the year before.

Margaret's power did overcome Billie Jean. Even in defeat, however, the nineteen year old from Long Beach had plenty of glory.

Doing What She Had to Do

After a poor showing at Wimbledon in 1964, Billie Jean knew she must do something drastic to improve her game. Her studies at college were taking away her practice time, and she was not progressing in tennis as she hoped she would. She was offered an expense-paid trip to Australia for three months if she wanted an intense and concentrated course in tennis. She talked it over with her boyfriend, Larry King, whom she had been dating for over a year.

''You can't pass up this opportunity, Billie Jean,'' he said.

21

"I don't know. By quitting school, I will be announcing that I want to become number one in the whole world. If I don't succeed, people will laugh at me," she argued. "But I guess I will take my chances and go."

She quit school, packed her bags, said goodbye to Larry, and left for Australia.

Tough going at Wimbledon

There a former top tennis player named Mervyn Rose
worked with her for eight hours a day. He taught her ways
to put more control in her shots, more power and variety
in her serve, and more thought into her whole game.When
she played in some Australian tournaments, the new
serve Mr. Rose was teaching her caused trouble, and she
lost a lot of games.

"Go back to your old serve," her friends suggested.
"You know you can win with that one."

She was tempted to do just that, but she remembered
that she also lost with her old serve. Mr. Rose convinced
her that she would, in the long run, do better if she
followed his advice. She trusted what he said and went to
work mastering her new serve.

Happy newlyweds, September 17, 1965

After three months she returned home and met Margaret Smith Court, newly married, at Forest Hills, the place of the United States championships. Billie Jean again lost to Margaret, still number one in the world. But Margaret admitted that she had played the best game of her life to beat Billie Jean.

Billie Jean Moffitt and Larry King were married in the fall of 1965 when he had one year of college and three years of law school ahead of him. Billie Jean gave some thought to giving up tennis for marriage, but Larry encouraged her to forget that idea.

''It is shameful if people do not use their talent,'' he said. ''In fact, it is the worst thing in the world.''

6

Number One

By the time Wimbledon of 1966 came around, Billie Jean was almost totally unbeaten in United States tennis tournaments. Her face, chubby and showing her many feelings, was a familiar one at Wimbledon where she had played the previous five years. She was still less powerful than some women and less ladylike and graceful than others. However, as a gutsy scrambler and fighter, she was considered number one.

Defeating the top women players that year, she made winning look easy. Maria Bueno from Brazil, who had her share of Wimbledon victories behind her, became Billie Jean's opponent in the important final game. The game was important because the United States had not won a singles trophy for four years.

"Simple," said Billie Jean as she won her first singles tournament, proving that she was tops in the world of tennis.

Jumping for joy after winning her first Wimbledon championship

After her victory, a committee named her the number one tennis player in the world. What a proud moment! But a second committee reversed the decision and said there were two "number ones." The committee stated that she had to share the number one billing with Nancy Richey.

Billie Jean resented that decision and asked, "Why should what you earn on a tennis court be taken away by people who have not even seen you play?"

It was a fair question.

The Triple Crown

In 1967 an aggressive and powerful Billie Jean came to Wimbledon to defend her title. She was about to prove in no uncertain terms that she was queen of the courts.

With over 300,000 spectators in attendance, more than ever before, and with three networks televising the historical event, Billie Jean King defended and kept her title as women's singles champion. With Rosemary Casals as her partner in the doubles final, and with Owen Davidson as partner in the mixed doubles final, two more trophies came into her possession after victorious matches. She had won a triple crown! No one person had won in all three categories at Wimbledon since 1951.

Billie Jean and partner Rosemary Casals in doubles tournament

Billie Jean has armful of trophies after winning the Triple Crown in 1967

In the United States championship games at Forest Hills, New York, she again won the trophies in all three categories. Another record! It had been twenty-eight years since a woman had won three titles at Wimbledon and three at Forest Hills in the same year.

She was named Outstanding Woman Athlete of 1967, and sports writers agreed that she ranked among the top women tennis players of history.

In an interview where she explained her success, she said, "One must never give up. You've got to want to win in tennis and be very, very competitive."

8

Going "Pro"

In 1967 Billie Jean was being listened to. She was speaking out for top to bottom changes in tennis.

"The image of tennis shouldn't be so sissy. Why shouldn't people shout? They pay money for their tickets, and they should be able to express themselves if they wish. Why do we always have to wear white? The scoring system is too complicated. The refereeing is ridiculous." She had lots to say.

In 1968 Wimbledon was opened to professional players as well as to amateurs. Players were professionals or "pros" if they played for money rather than for cups or other trophies. Amateurs were supposed to be playing for love of the game, but most amateurs had their expenses paid for them. Sometimes the "expense money" was more than the professionals received in their pay checks. So the money distinction was objectionable to Billie Jean.

With husband, Larry, at London airport after Wimbledon tournament

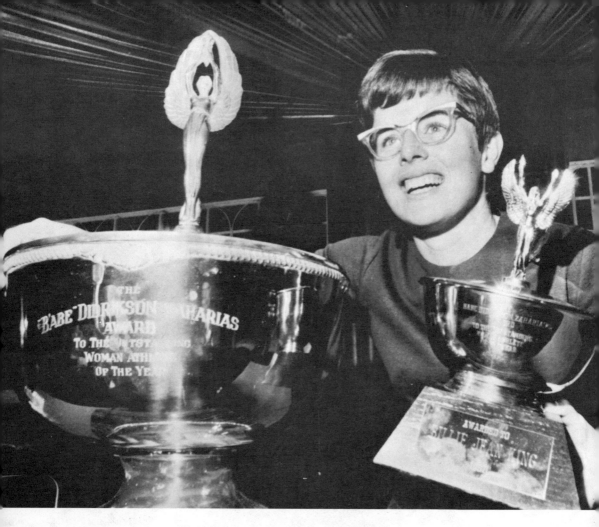

Receiving Babe Didrikson Zaharias award as Outstanding Woman Athlete of 1967

''Even college stars who receive scholarships are really professionals,'' she argued. ''And pros love the game as much as amateurs do. They give their lives to it.''

In 1968 she herself turned pro, signed a contract for $45,000 a year, and began touring the country, playing before crowds, giving great exhibitions of tennis at its best.

Defending the Title

Billie Jean, now accepted as one of the finest players in the history of tennis, had to struggle to defend her title against champions of other years.

By 1968 she was no longer "Little Miss Moffitt," the young newcomer who had been cheered. She was twenty-four year old Mrs. King the champion, and people were anxious to challenge her. Some were critical of her, jealous of her.

She had, since becoming a professional, been on tours, and she was often exhausted! One night she felt completely fed up. She flew home to California, slept for twenty-one hours straight, saw a doctor who discovered a medical problem, and was back on the tour within a week. The doctor prescribed lots of sleep and no tension. Imagine!

With her parents, Betty and Bill Moffitt, and husband, Larry, Billie Jean watches for a change.

Billie Jean's desire had been to get to the top, then reach out and help people, but she found herself somewhat isolated. She continued to talk with anyone who would listen, being critical of tennis and how it was run. Sometimes she annoyed people with her outspoken views, but she was known as a true star who drew interested people to the courts and increased the popularity of tennis.

Discussing the upcoming match at Wimbledon in 1968, she admitted, ''I am playing my worst tennis in three years. If I win, it will be on fight.''

Bill and Betty Moffitt were full of pride as they saw their daughter win the women's singles title for the third straight year. That evening, as she danced the first dance at the victory ball with Rod Laver, the men's champion, they knew Billie Jean had achieved her dream.

36

Billie Jean dancing with Rod Laver at the Lawn Tennis Association Ball — they had won the singles championships.

10

Breaking Another Record

A fall at Wimbledon in 1970 made a knee operation necessary. A first knee operation had been successful a few years before, and Billie Jean hoped for the best. She was slowed down for awhile, but just for a little while. Soon she was up again.

In 1970 she helped organize the Virginia Slims tennis tour for women only. The slogan for Virginia Slims cigarettes was "You've come a long way, Baby." Indeed the women had come a long way. Billie Jean had been anxious to help organize the tour because she was tired of women's matches being merely colorful sidelines for the matches between men. The women had to publicize their own tour and make it a success without the help of men.

Their tour helped focus on excellence of play, not on the details and etiquette of tennis with which so many people identified the game.

A fall during a long match with Margaret Court in 1970

Billie Jean in action in 1970

"We're trying to get away from the clubby, rich, and white atmosphere and bring the game to the people," Billie Jean explained.

Tennis was taking hold of America with over 500,000 players taking up the sport each year. Eleven and one half million players were participating by 1971. Over five thousand new courts were being built each year. Requiring very little equipment and being good exercise, tennis had an appeal for young and old alike.

Billie Jean celebrates being the first woman athlete to win more than $100,000 in one season.

After staggering along for centuries, being somewhat limited to rich people, tennis was finally being brought to everyone by the understanding of the greatness of the game. From an unknown sport, it had risen to startling popularity. Tennis, anyone? Yes, for everyone!

After having the best tennis year of her life and going further than any other woman athlete to date by earning over $100,000, Billie Jean lost a semifinal match at Wimbledon in 1971 to Evonne Goolagong. Evonne, a young woman from Australia, went on to win the championship and be named the world's number one tennis player. That hurt Billie Jean!

41

Chapter 11

Up Again

By 1972 she was back at Wimbledon to win the title she had lost the year before. At age 28 she called herself the ''old lady of tennis.'' The spectators loved youth, and the young tennis players were getting most of the attention.

One player, Rosie Casals, was ordered off the court for wearing too much color (plus an ad for Virginia Slims on the pocket of her dress). Tennis may have come a long way, but not quite far enough.

Billie Jean was anxious to play Evonne again. The spectators were cheering for Evonne, who had great speed, strength, and youth. Evonne's youth did generate a magic spell, but Billie Jean's skill won the game. She trounced Evonne and threw her racquet in the air. With the American, French, and Wimbledon championships under her belt, she was undisputed queen, and her name would go down in sports history. Billie Jean marched around the court in triumph, and the spectators proclaimed her queen once again.

SPORTS ILLUSTRATED Sportswoman of the Year, 1972 — with her is James Wooden, son of John Wooden, SPORTS ILLUSTRATED Sportsman of the Year, 1972

Sports Illustrated named her the 1972 Sportswoman of the Year. In an interview with the writers of the magazine, she said, ''Tennis teaches us about life. We can't always have things go our own way. We win some and lose some. We're sometimes up and sometimes down. That's what sport is all about. That is what life is all about.''

Evonne Goolagong

Billie Jean King at Wimbledon

12

Men Better than Women?

Since 1971, a man named Bobby Riggs was often stating publicly, ''Men are better than women in everything, especially in tennis.''

Many people probably thought the same way, but Bobby spoke out for all to hear. He had been a big tennis star at Wimbledon in 1939 and loved the attention he had received at that time.

After his stardom in tennis had stopped, he missed the publicity and center stage. He seemed to be mad, and maybe even a bit jealous, that women were earning more money than he had when he was at his best. So he started making a lot of silly statements.

''Men are naturally better tennis players than women. In everything men are better than women. In fact, I bet the very best woman tennis player cannot beat an old man like me.'' He was 55 years old.

Bobby Riggs with Billie Jean King

He taunted Billie Jean to get her to agree to a match with him. She refused.

One day Margaret Smith Court accepted Bobby's challenge, and a well publicized match was set for Mother's Day, 1973.

Margaret was a great tennis player, no doubt about
that. But she made at least two mistakes: first, she let
Bobby get on her nerves as he kept telling her how the
women of the whole world were depending on her to win;
and second, she did not really study Bobby's tennis game.
She came to the match unprepared for the way he played.

Margaret was so nervous and tense on Mother's Day
that she could not do anything right on the court. Her
game was a complete disaster, and, of course, Bobby
Riggs won an easy victory. He gloated and said that he
had proven his point: men were better than women, and
women tennis players were paid too much for what they
were worth.

Billie Jean, of course, knew he was all wet and decided
she had to play him, beat him, and make him eat his
words.

So she agreed to a match after Labor Day, 1973. Then
she was off to Wimbledon again.

48

13 Chapter

Another Triple Crown

People are fickle, and their feelings change. At Wimbledon, Billie Jean found they were not cheering for her anymore, but that was to be expected. She remembered her first years as a young unknown player when she was a favorite of the crowd and she had thrilled the spectators with her upset of Margaret Smith. Again in 1973 the crowds were behind the younger players, especially Chris Evert who was an upcoming teenage tennis wonder.

In the semifinals, young Chris beat older Margaret Smith Court; and older Billie Jean beat younger Evonne Goolagong. Then for the first time since 1957, two American women were in the finals. Chris was in the finals for the first time, and Billie Jean for the eighth. Of course, the crowd was openly behind "Chrissie."

Billie Jean did mind the cheers were not for her, but she tried not to show it. She really wanted to win. In fact her weight had been such a problem that she had gone so far as to give up ice cream until after Wimbledon. Ice cream had always been one of her greatest weaknesses.

49

Billie Jean bites a tennis ball after missing a shot

Victorious Billie Jean, Triple Crown winner, with Chris Evert after the championship match, Wimbledon, 1973

The first set played was termed the very best in Billie Jean's entire career. When the final set was over, victory had come to Billie Jean and with it her fifth singles championship. To make the tournament complete, she gained her ninth doubles and third mixed doubles titles. For the second time in her life she had won the triple crown. Billie Jean King was indeed queen.

14

Proving a Point

In 1973 Billie Jean founded the Women's Tennis Association and was its first president. With her husband Larry as her business manager, she was busy. She owned sports shops and camps, and she was endorsing racquets, shoes, and tennis clothes. She was asked to coach a new tennis team, the Philadelphia Freedoms, and was under pressure as the only woman coach of a major professional team.

She was speaking out against the inequality of funds given to schools for boys' and girls' athletic programs. It had always been taken for granted that men's sports should receive many times the money given to women's sports. Billie Jean told a Senate subcommittee about the problem. The senators respected her and listened to her.

Billie Jean had many things to do, but the Bobby Riggs thing had to be settled. September 20 was the date selected.

Speaking before a Senate Education Subcommittee in 1973

Billie Jean had been saying, ''Women in tennis are as good as men and should be given equal opportunities.''

Bobby was saying, ''Prove it. Women are worse than men players. You are even worse than I am, and I'm an old man!''

No one knew whether Bobby believed what he was
saying. Many suspected that he just wanted center stage
again, after 30 years. He did get the stage. He was
interviewed for television, his picture appeared on the
cover of several national magazines, and his name became
an everyday household word.

Playing for keeps, September 20, 1973

The winner!

Billie Jean King's name became well known in every household, too. People who were not sure whether she was a lady halfback or a golf star saw a tennis match on September 20 which made her famous forever.

About 30,000 spectators were on hand, and forty million others watched on television in the United States and overseas by satellite. They all saw a woman in action give a dazzling exhibition of tennis at its best. Of course, she defeated Bobby Riggs easily, and the spectators went wild.

What the spectators may not have known when they saw her that night was just how far Billie Jean had come from the day she could not be in a photo because she was not dressed properly. Someday, perhaps, they would realize how she had furthered the causes of women, tennis, and women in tennis.

Chapter 15

Into the Future

By 1974 the biggest news in tennis was the formation of the World Team Tennis League. Americans had always liked the idea of playing in teams, and Billie Jean worked long and hard to help get the WTT on its feet.

Team tennis is different from court tennis. Marching bands are sometimes present, spectators are encouraged to cheer, and score-keeping has been streamlined from the standard way. Most significant of all, the women players compete on an equal basis with men, sharing the same glamour, prestige, and big-money contracts.

Woman of the Year, 1974, Sports Category: Billie Jean King

In early June, Billie Jean, acting as coach and player, came with her Philadelphia Freedoms to meet her Wimbledon doubles partner, Owen Davidson, and the team he was coaching, the Minnesota Buckskins. She generated so much excitement that the WTT record-breaking crowd of 10,658 at the sports arena in Minneapolis gave her a standing ovation.

In a Virginia Slims tournament, 1974

During that same week, Chris Evert was in the Rome Open tournament adding another victory to her already lengthy list.

At Wimbledon 1974, Billie Jean was the top seeded woman. She and Owen Davidson did win the mixed doubles title, her eighteenth at Wimbledon, but, alas, she was beat out in the singles quarter finals by Olga Morozova.

Chris Evert, hottest ever, was in the midst of a ten tournament, fifty-six game winning streak, and Wimbledon was hers! Her fiance, Jimmy Connors, won the men's singles, and the spectators were thrilled watching the young sweethearts dance the first dance at the victory ball.

Named honorary fire chief in Philadelphia

Tennis fans wondered whether Billie Jean meant it when she came to Wimbledon in 1975 announcing her plans to retire. She was thirty-one and considered by some to be the "old lady of tennis."

She had been busy with her new magazine, **womenSports** and was committed to helping women in sports achieve equality in opportunity and pay. She had switched her World Team Tennis allegiance to the New York Sets and continued as president of the Women's Tennis Association.

Chris Evert, the women's defending champion, won the Virginia Slims tournament and held major titles in Paris and Rome. She had not lost a match since April and was favored to capture the singles title for the second year in a row.

Billie Jean made up for her 1974 loss to Olga Morozova by defeating her in the quarter finals. The semi-final match with Chris Evert was a real upset, and triumphant Billie Jean gained the finals for the ninth time in her life, matching the record of the all-time great, Helen Wills Moody. As she left the center court, she heard the crowd enthusiastically applauding.

In 39 minutes Billie Jean King defeated Evonne Goolagong Cawley for the singles title. No game had been easier or more lopsided, and no victory had ever been more precious to her.

With that victory, Billie Jean earned her nineteenth Wimbledon title, tying another record held by Elizabeth Ryan. She had few tennis worlds left to conquer.

"What a way to end my career. It's as close as I've come to a perfect match," the jubilant winner said in an interview. "I want to go out on a high. It's time for the youngsters to take over."

Evonne was resigned. "There was nothing I could do."

Giving pointers to a future champion

As the crowds cheered, Billie Jean's life flashed before her. She remembered telling her mother when she was five years old, "Mom, I think I've got something special going for me."

Her mother had answered, "Do what you have to do."

Billie Jean remembered her hours of practice, her victories and losses, her opposition and support. She had always been controversial. She realized that she had a wonderful and unique opportunity of living with the very changes in tennis she had helped bring about.

She had done and would continue doing what she had to do.

Anything is possible for Billie Jean

CAROL BAUER CHURCH is a graduate of the College of St. Catherine in St. Paul, Minnesota. She is a former school teacher and lives with her husband Jim and daughter Laura. She is currently working on additional titles for the **Focus on Famous Women Series**.